Athletes Who Made a Difference

JESSE OWENS

Blake Hoena
illustrated by David Shephard

Graphic Universe™ • Minneapolis

Graphic Universe™
An imprint of Lerner Publishing Group, Inc.
241 First Avenue North
Minneapolis, MN 55401 USA

For reading levels and more information, look up this title at www.lernerbooks.com.

Main body text set in CCDaveGibbonsLower
Typeface provided by Comicraft

Photo Acknowledgments
The photos in this book are used with the permission of: Acme News Photos/Wikimedia Commons, p. 28 (left); Library of Congress via pingnews/Flickr, p. 28 (right).

Library of Congress Cataloging-in-Publication Data

Names: Hoena, B. A., author. | Shephard, David (Illustrator), illustrator. | Graphic Universe (Firm)
Title: Jesse Owens : athletes who made a difference / Blake Hoena ; [illustrated by] David Shephard.
Other titles: Making a difference. Athletes who are changing the world.
Description: Minneapolis : Graphic Universe an imprint of Lerner Publishing Group, Inc., 2020. | Series: Athletes who made a difference | Includes bibliographical references and index. | Audience: Ages: 8–12 years | Audience: Grades: 4–6 | Summary: "Jesse Owens smashed records throughout his track and field career. In 1936, he made history at the Olympic Games in Berlin, Germany. Owens won four gold medals, combating Adolf Hitler's message of Nazi superiority." — Provided by publisher.
Identifiers: LCCN 2019041857 (print) | LCCN 2019041858 (ebook) | ISBN 9781541578159 (Library Binding) | ISBN 9781728402956 (Paperback) | ISBN 9781541599444 (eBook)
Subjects: LCSH: Owens, Jesse, 1913–1980—Juvenile literature. | Track and field athletes—United States—Biography—Juvenile literature. | African American track and field athletes—Biography—Juvenile literature. | African Americans—Biography—Juvenile literature. | Olympics—Participation, American. | Olympic athletes—United States—Biography—Juvenile literature. | Olympic Games (11th : 1936 : Berlin, Germany)—Juvenile literature. | National socialism—Philosophy. | Racism—Germany—History—20th century.
Classification: LCC GV697.O9 H64 2020 (print) | LCC GV697.O9 (ebook) | DDC 796.42092 [B]—dc23

LC record available at https://lccn.loc.gov/2019041857
LC ebook record available at https://lccn.loc.gov/2019041858

Manufactured in the United States of America
1 – CG – 7/15/20

Table of Contents

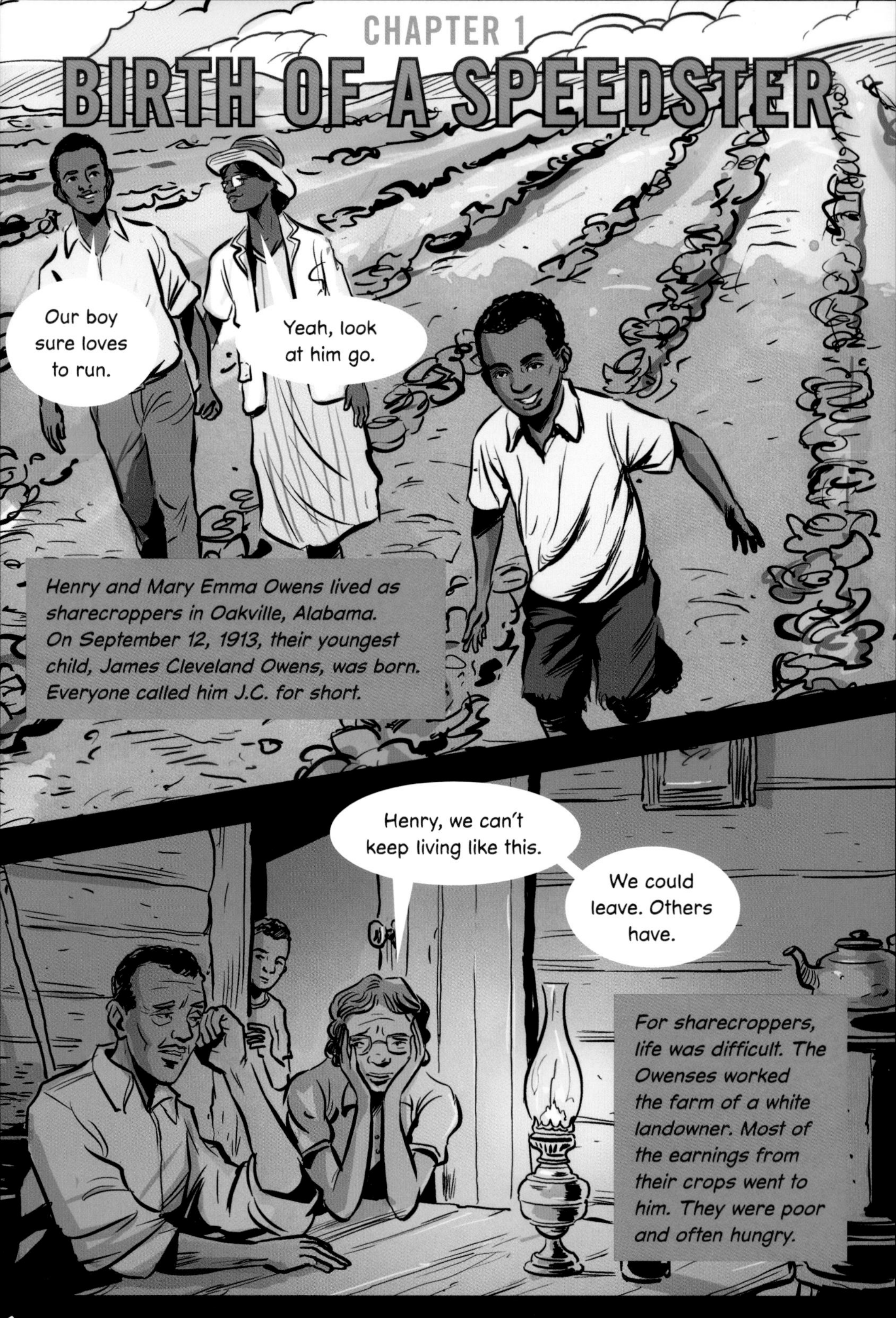
CHAPTER 1
BIRTH OF A SPEEDSTER
Our boy sure loves to run.
Yeah, look at him go.
Henry and Mary Emma Owens lived as sharecroppers in Oakville, Alabama. On September 12, 1913, their youngest child, James Cleveland Owens, was born. Everyone called him J.C. for short.
Henry, we can't keep living like this.
We could leave. Others have.
For sharecroppers, life was difficult. The Owenses worked the farm of a white landowner. Most of the earnings from their crops went to him. They were poor and often hungry.

In 1922, the Owenses left their home in Alabama. They were part of the Great Migration of African American families heading north in the hope of better lives.

Why are we moving to Cleveland?

That's where your sister Lillie lives. And maybe your father can find work in a factory.

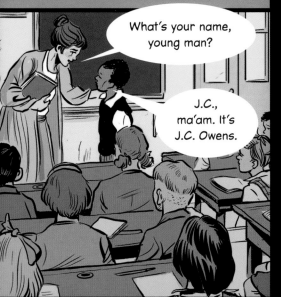

In Cleveland, Ohio, J.C. entered the first grade at Bolton Elementary.

What's your name, young man?

J.C., ma'am. It's J.C. Owens.

But the teacher misheard what J.C. said.

Class, we have a new student. Everybody welcome Jesse Owens.

From that day on, most people would know him as Jesse.

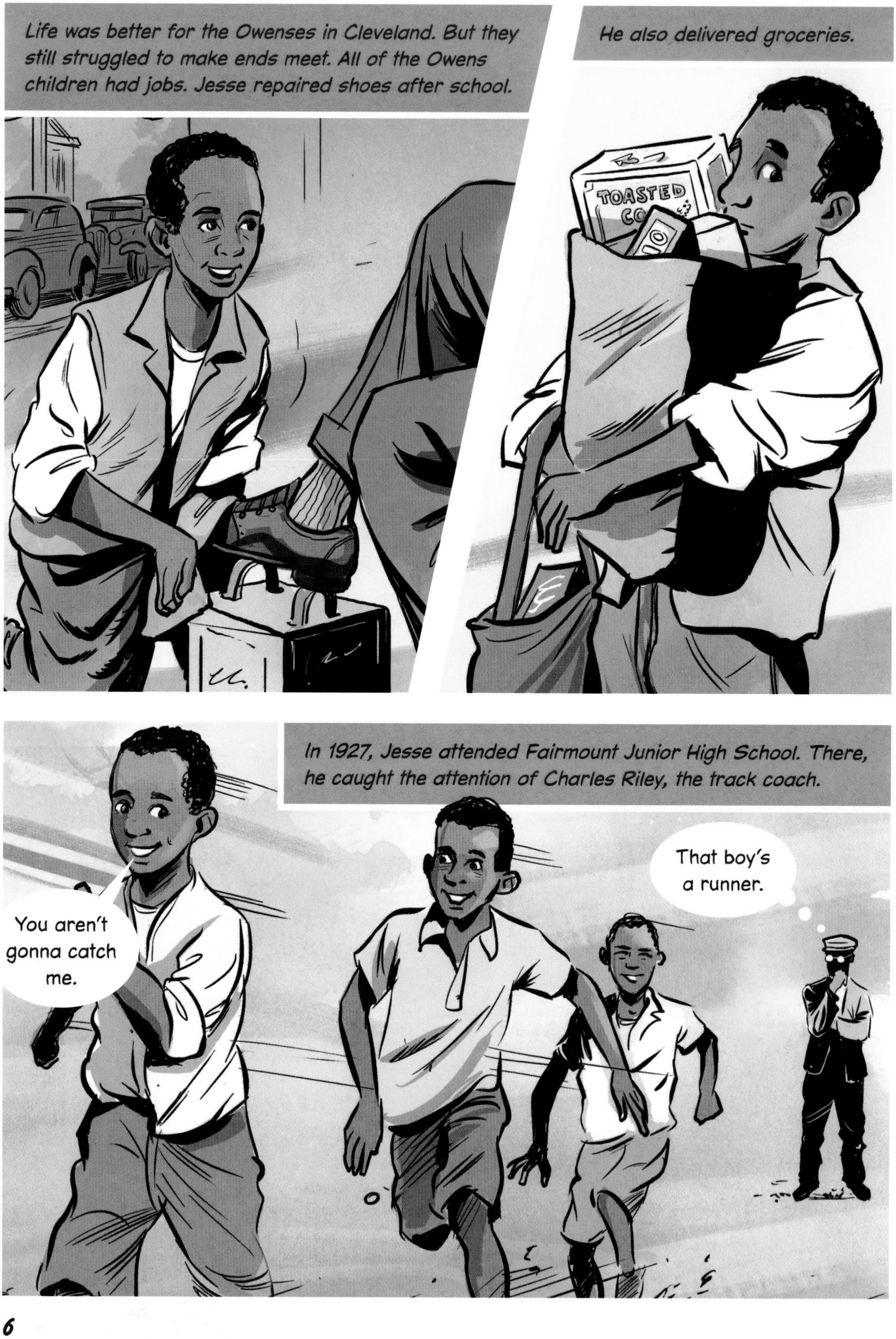
Life was better for the Owenses in Cleveland. But they still struggled to make ends meet. All of the Owens children had jobs. Jesse repaired shoes after school.
He also delivered groceries.
TOASTED
In 1927, Jesse attended Fairmount Junior High School. There, he caught the attention of Charles Riley, the track coach.
You aren't gonna catch me.
That boy's a runner.

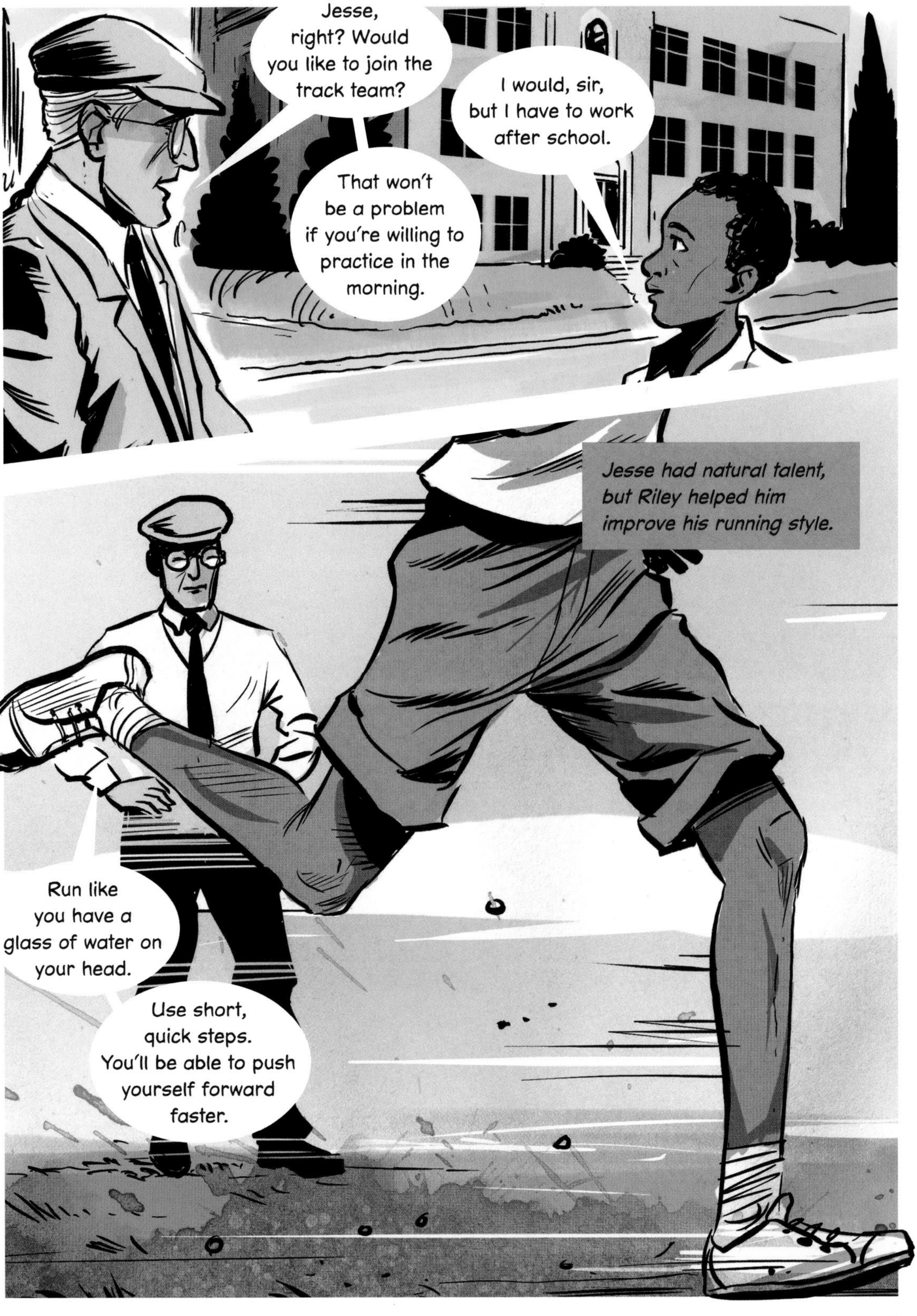
Jesse, right? Would you like to join the track team?
I would, sir, but I have to work after school.
That won't be a problem if you're willing to practice in the morning.
Jesse had natural talent, but Riley helped him improve his running style.
Run like you have a glass of water on your head.
Use short, quick steps. You'll be able to push yourself forward faster.

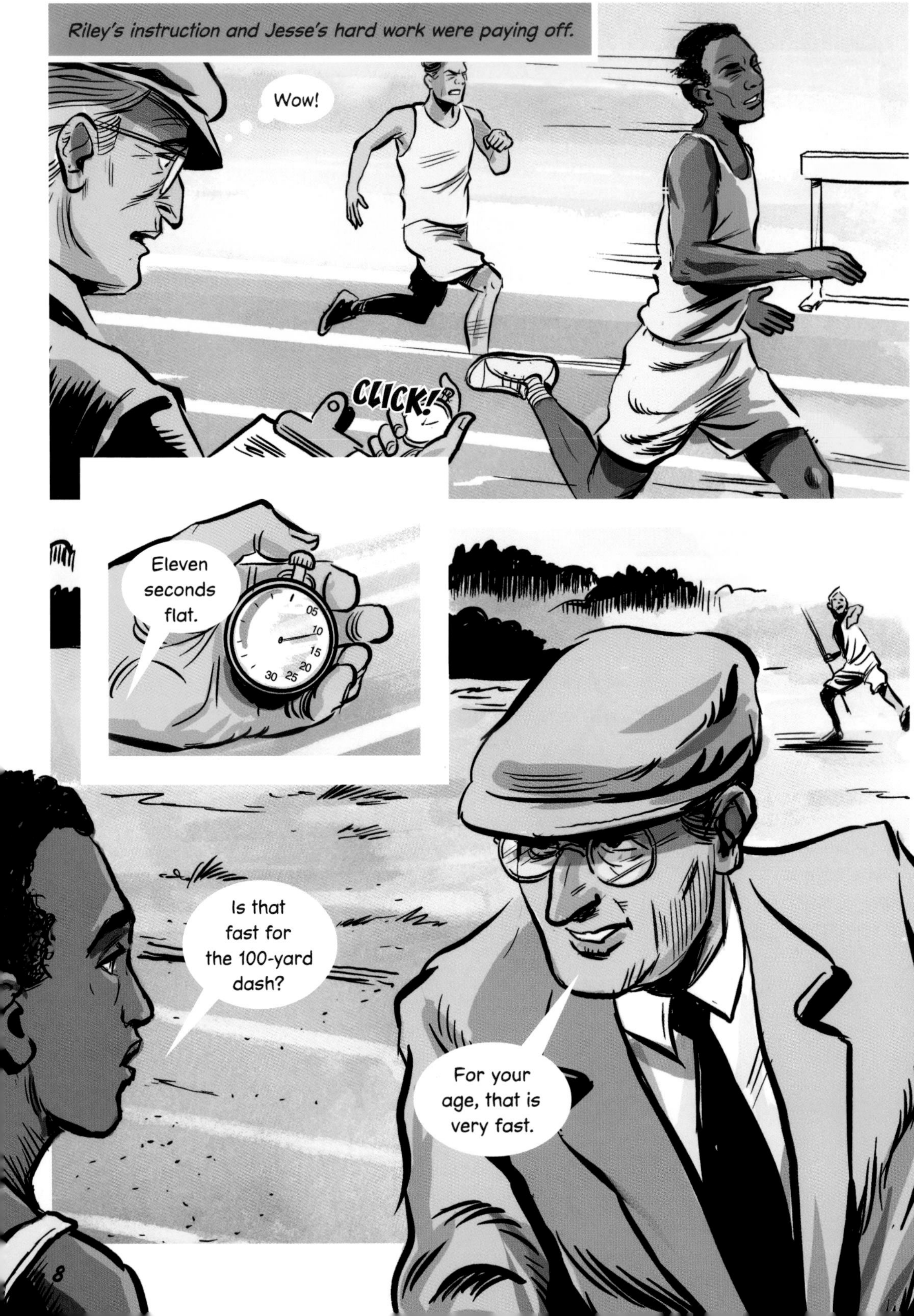
Riley's instruction and Jesse's hard work were paying off.
Wow!
CLICK!
Eleven seconds flat.
05
10
15
20
25
30
Is that fast for the 100-yard dash?
For your age, that is very fast.

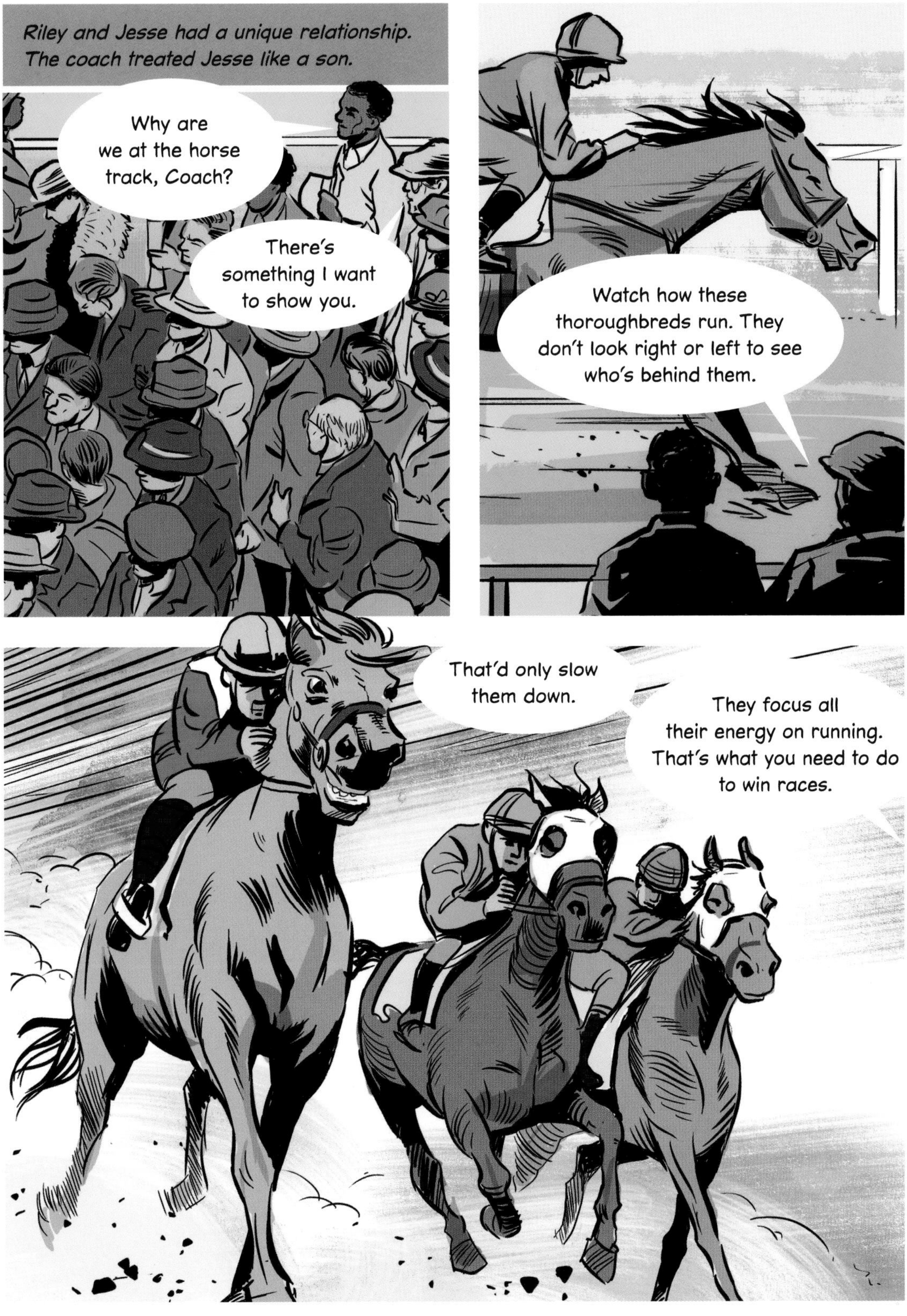
Riley and Jesse had a unique relationship. The coach treated Jesse like a son.
Why are we at the horse track, Coach?
There's something I want to show you.
Watch how these thoroughbreds run. They don't look right or left to see who's behind them.
That'd only slow them down.
They focus all their energy on running. That's what you need to do to win races.

CHAPTER 2

MAKING A NAME FOR HIMSELF

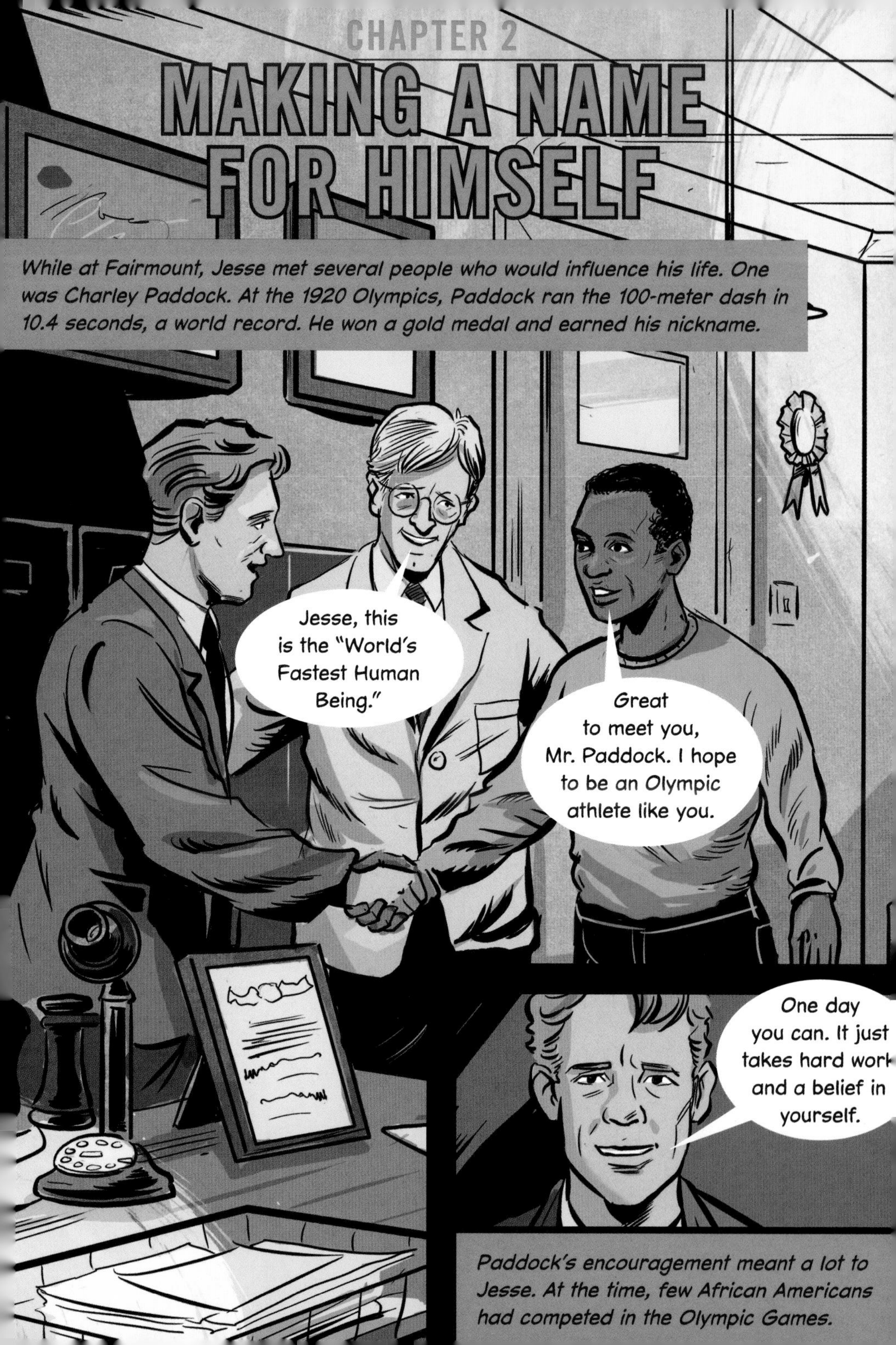

While at Fairmount, Jesse met several people who would influence his life. One was Charley Paddock. At the 1920 Olympics, Paddock ran the 100-meter dash in 10.4 seconds, a world record. He won a gold medal and earned his nickname.
Jesse, this is the "World's Fastest Human Being."
Great to meet you, Mr. Paddock. I hope to be an Olympic athlete like you.
One day you can. It just takes hard work and a belief in yourself.
Paddock's encouragement meant a lot to Jesse. At the time, few African Americans had competed in the Olympic Games.

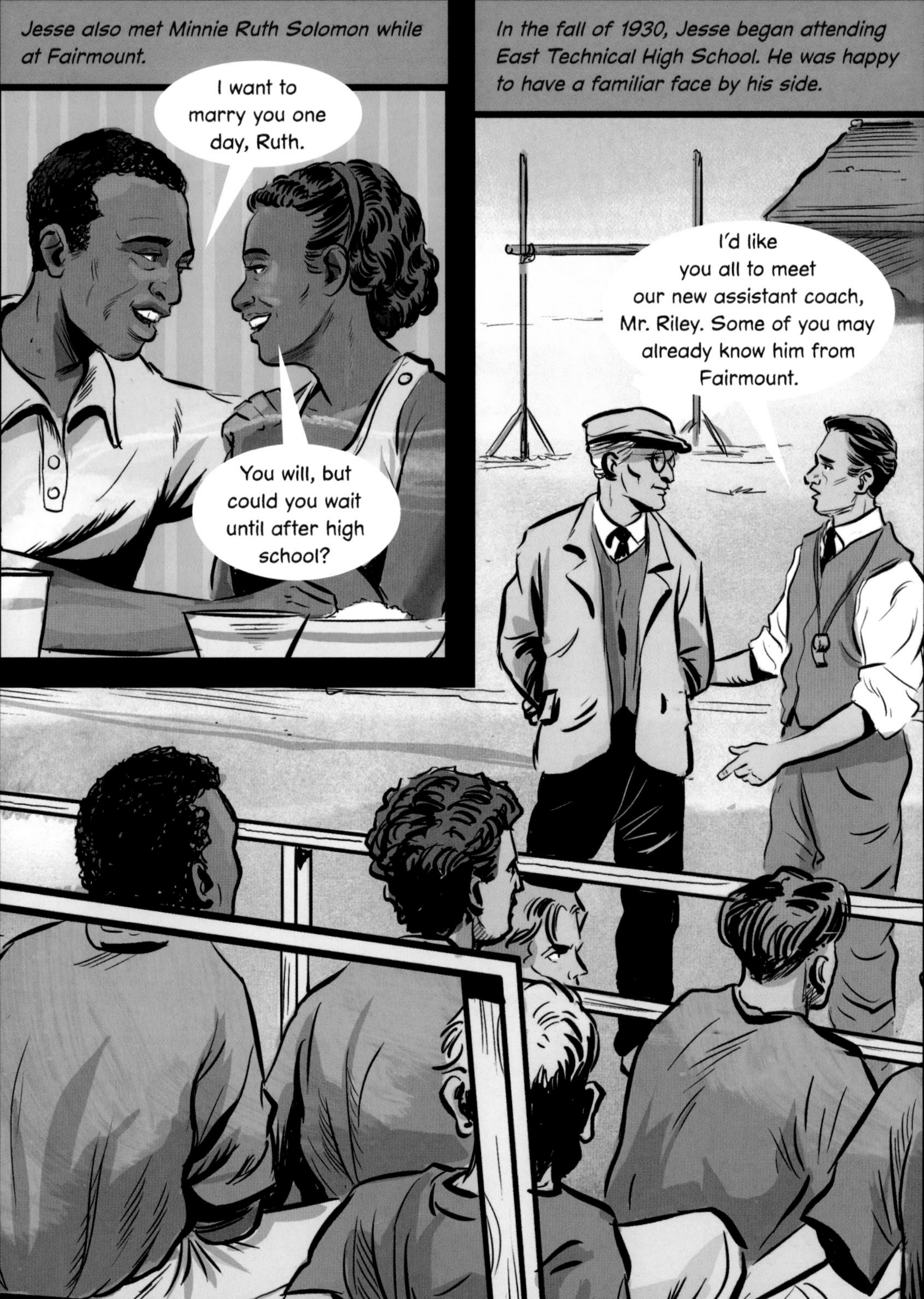
Jesse also met Minnie Ruth Solomon while at Fairmount.
I want to marry you one day, Ruth.
You will, but could you wait until after high school?
In the fall of 1930, Jesse began attending East Technical High School. He was happy to have a familiar face by his side.
I'd like you all to meet our new assistant coach, Mr. Riley. Some of you may already know him from Fairmount.

Jesse's high school years were eventful. During one track meet, he nearly broke Paddock's world record for the 100-meter dash.

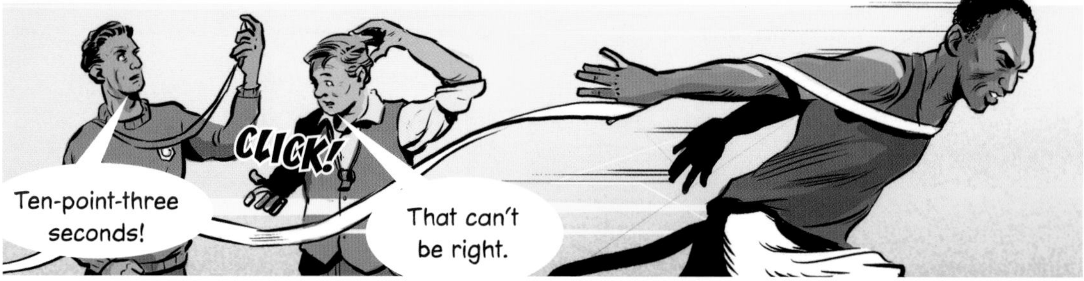
CLICK!
Ten-point-three seconds!
That can't be right.

Race officials did not allow the record. They said a strong tailwind aided Jesse too much. But Jesse was invited to Illinois try out for the 1932 Olympics. There, he raced older, more experienced runners.

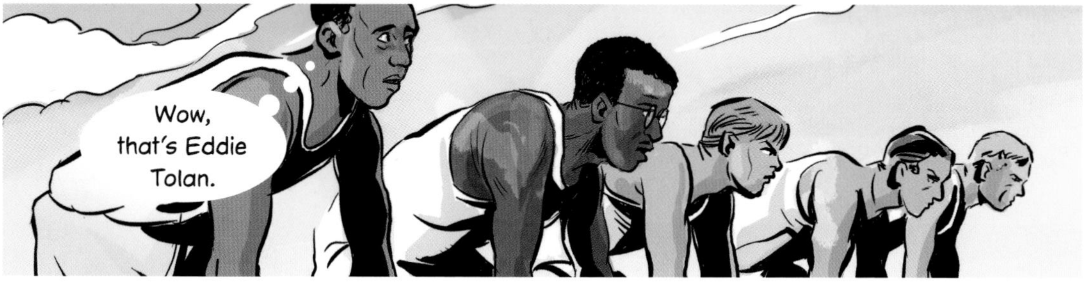
Wow, that's Eddie Tolan.

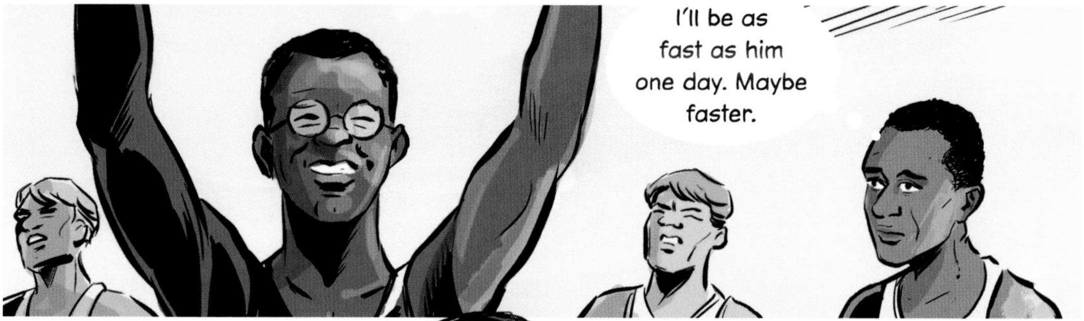
I'll be as fast as him one day. Maybe faster.

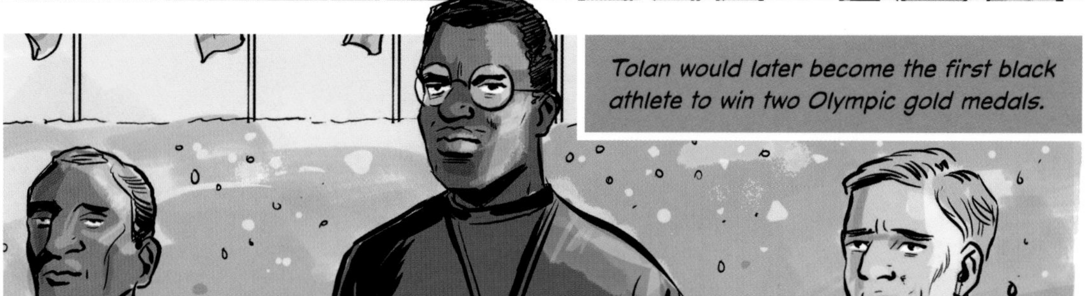
Tolan would later become the first black athlete to win two Olympic gold medals.

While Jesse was disappointed that he didn't qualify for the Olympics, he had reason to celebrate back home.

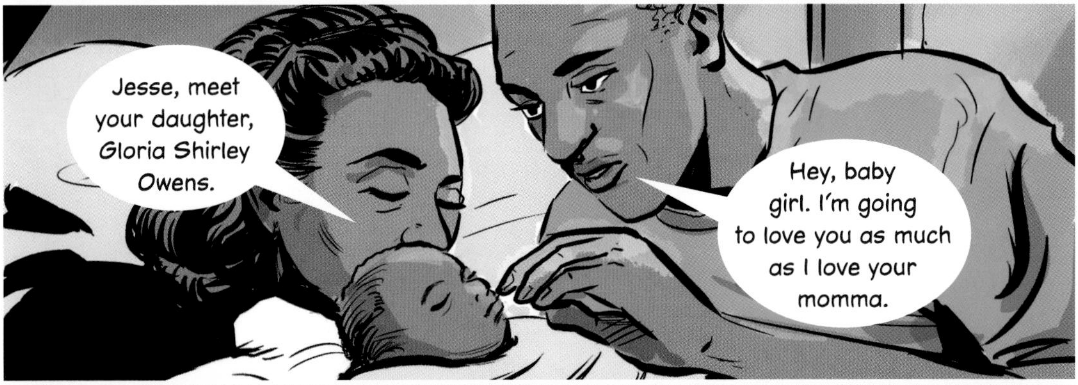
Jesse, meet your daughter, Gloria Shirley Owens.
Hey, baby girl. I'm going to love you as much as I love your momma.

Jesse and Ruth would marry in 1935. They would go on to have two more daughters, Marlene (1939) and Beverly (1940).

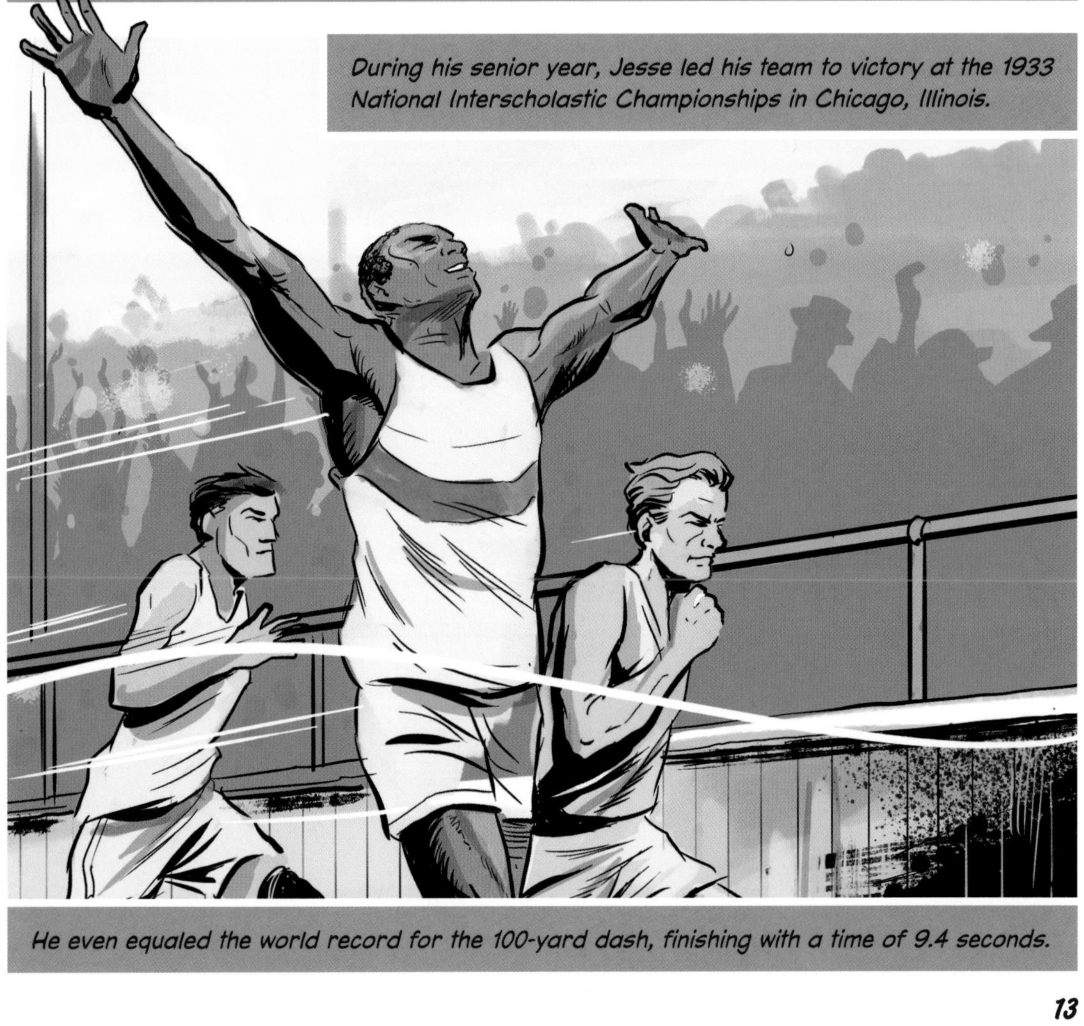
During his senior year, Jesse led his team to victory at the 1933 National Interscholastic Championships in Chicago, Illinois.

He even equaled the world record for the 100-yard dash, finishing with a time of 9.4 seconds.

CHAPTER 3
THE GREATEST 45 MINUTES IN SPORTS

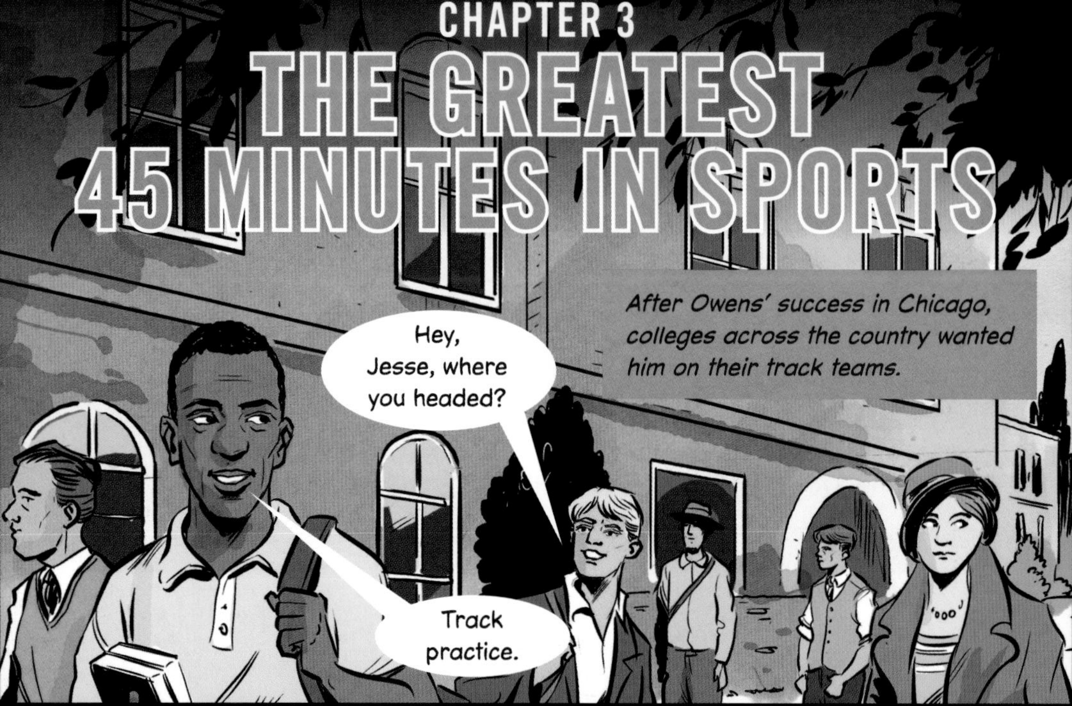
After Owens' success in Chicago, colleges across the country wanted him on their track teams.
Hey, Jesse, where you headed?
Track practice.

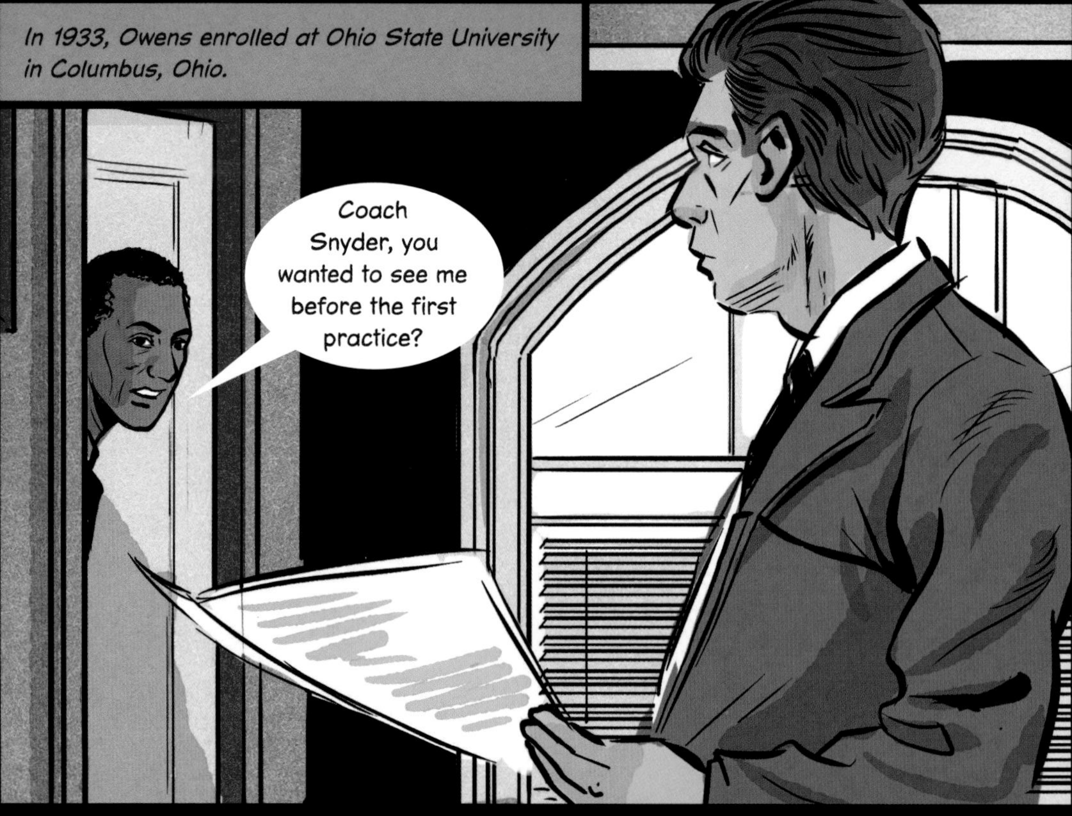
In 1933, Owens enrolled at Ohio State University in Columbus, Ohio.
Coach Snyder, you wanted to see me before the first practice?

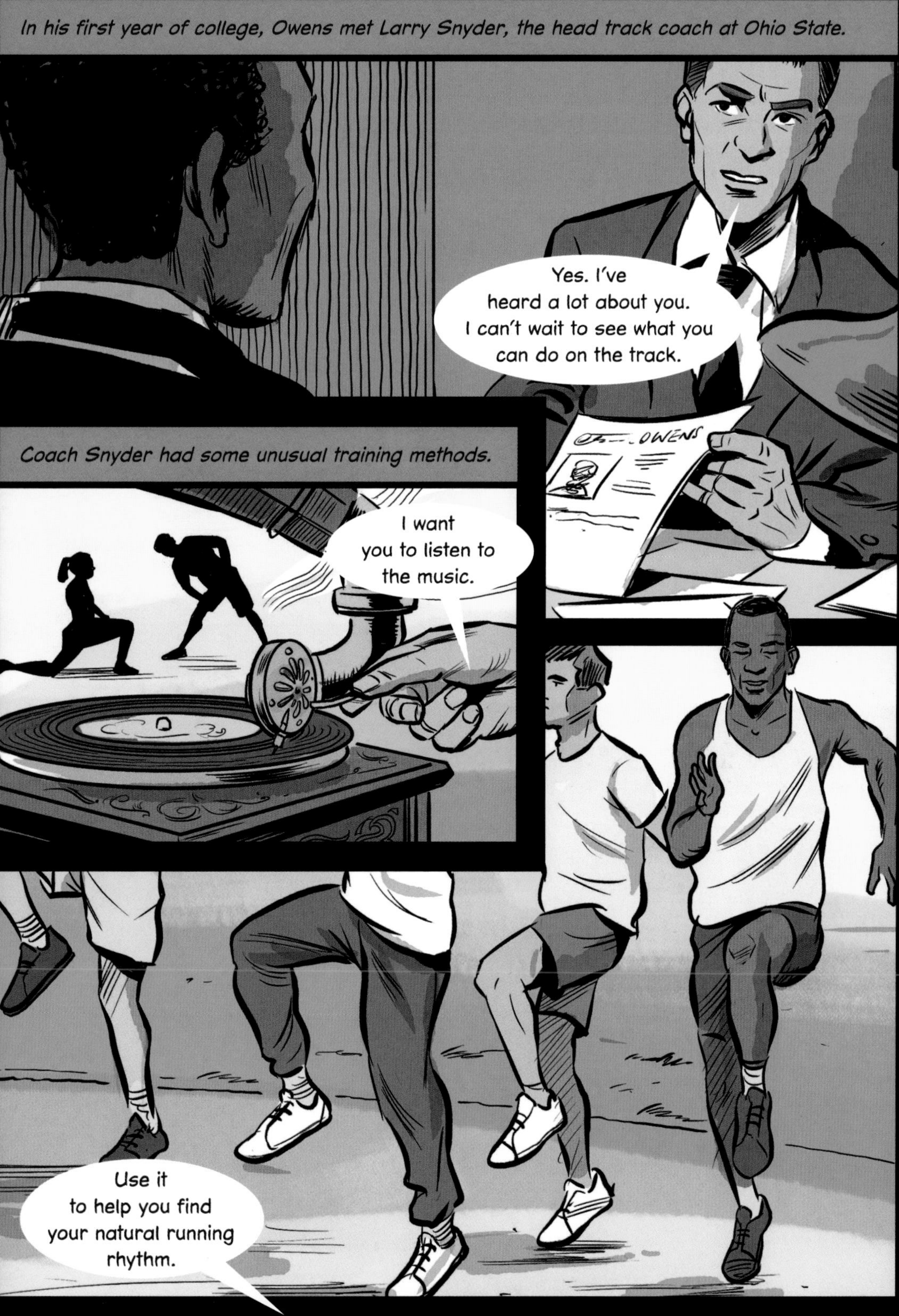
In his first year of college, Owens met Larry Snyder, the head track coach at Ohio State.
Yes. I've heard a lot about you. I can't wait to see what you can do on the track.
OWENS
Coach Snyder had some unusual training methods.
I want you to listen to the music.
Use it to help you find your natural running rhythm.

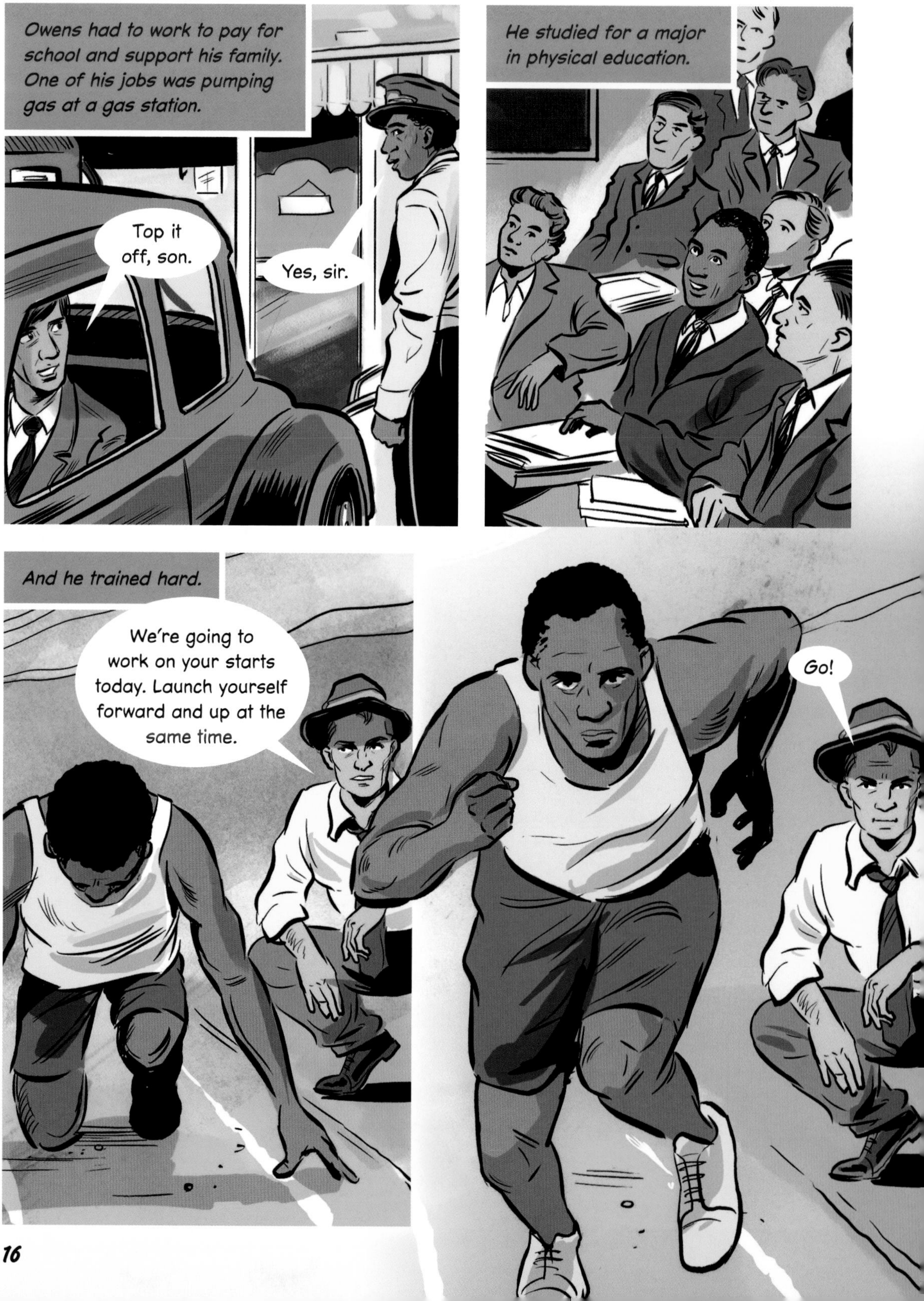

Owens had to work to pay for school and support his family. One of his jobs was pumping gas at a gas station.
Top it off, son.
Yes, sir.
He studied for a major in physical education.
And he trained hard.
We're going to work on your starts today. Launch yourself forward and up at the same time.
Go!

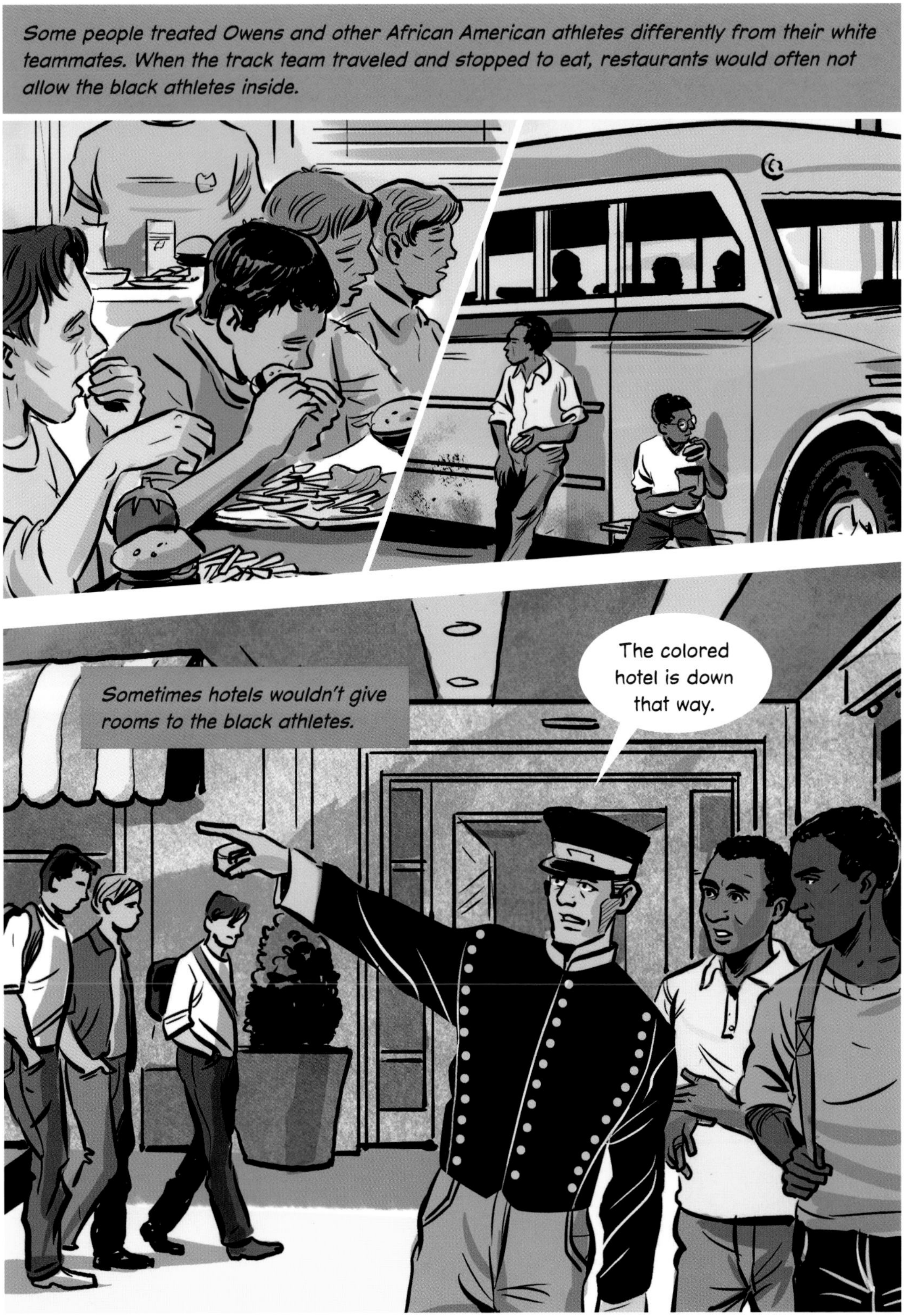
Some people treated Owens and other African American athletes differently from their white teammates. When the track team traveled and stopped to eat, restaurants would often not allow the black athletes inside.
Sometimes hotels wouldn't give rooms to the black athletes.
The colored hotel is down that way.

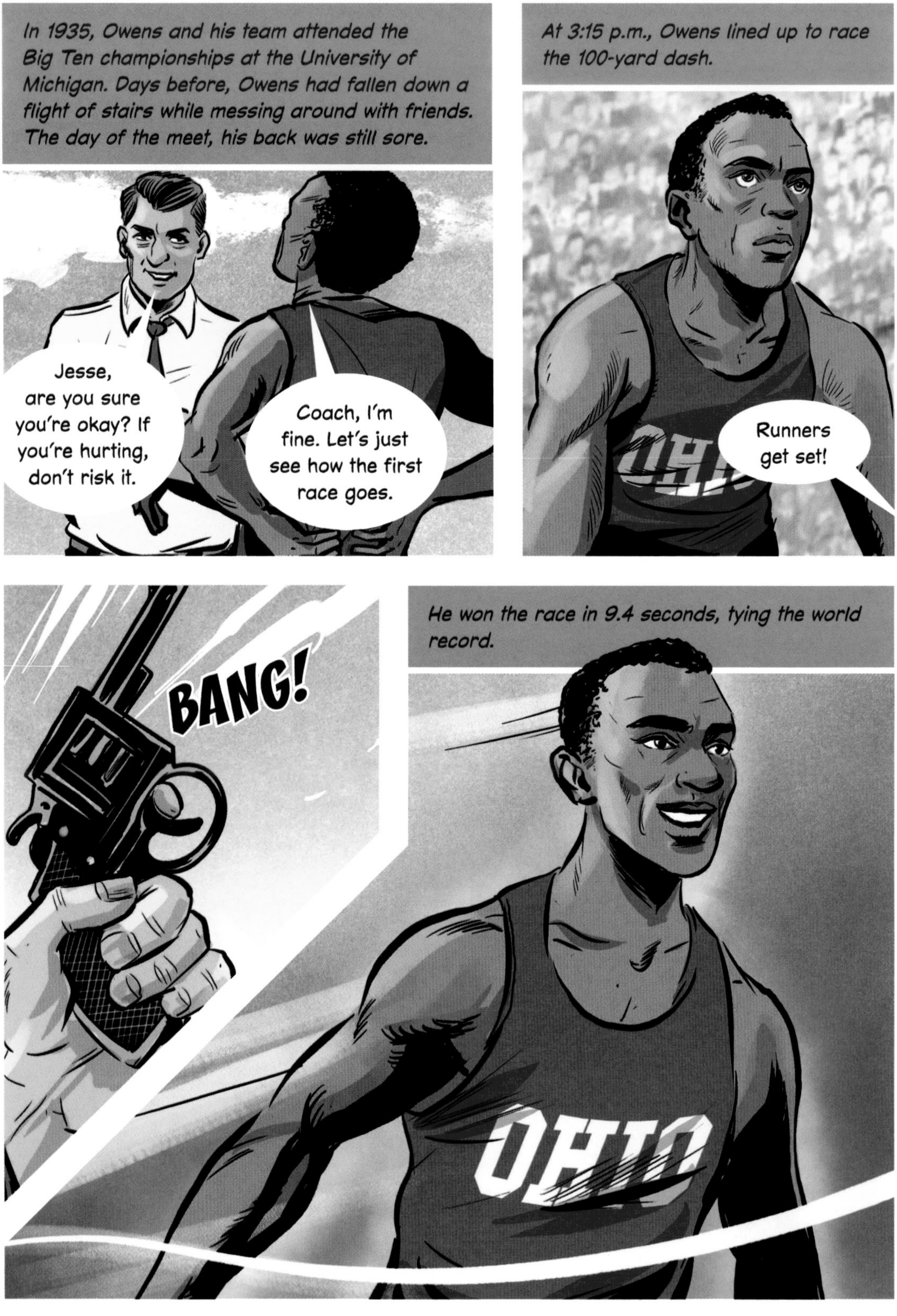
In 1935, Owens and his team attended the Big Ten championships at the University of Michigan. Days before, Owens had fallen down a flight of stairs while messing around with friends. The day of the meet, his back was still sore.
Jesse, are you sure you're okay? If you're hurting, don't risk it.
Coach, I'm fine. Let's just see how the first race goes.
At 3:15 p.m., Owens lined up to race the 100-yard dash.
OHIO
Runners get set!
BANG!
He won the race in 9.4 seconds, tying the world record.
OHIO

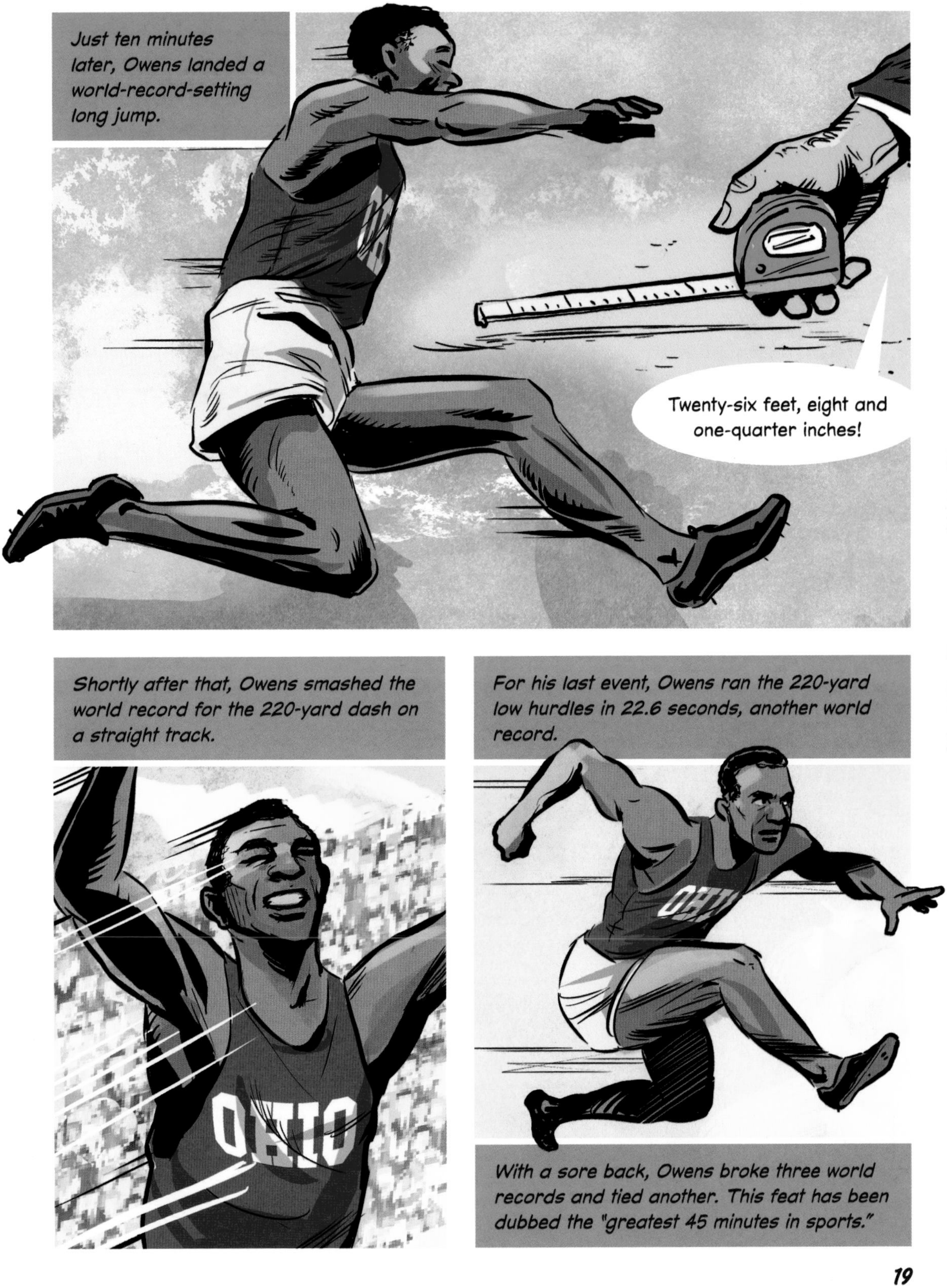
Just ten minutes later, Owens landed a world-record-setting long jump.
Twenty-six feet, eight and one-quarter inches!
Shortly after that, Owens smashed the world record for the 220-yard dash on a straight track.
OHIO
For his last event, Owens ran the 220-yard low hurdles in 22.6 seconds, another world record.
OHIO
With a sore back, Owens broke three world records and tied another. This feat has been dubbed the "greatest 45 minutes in sports."

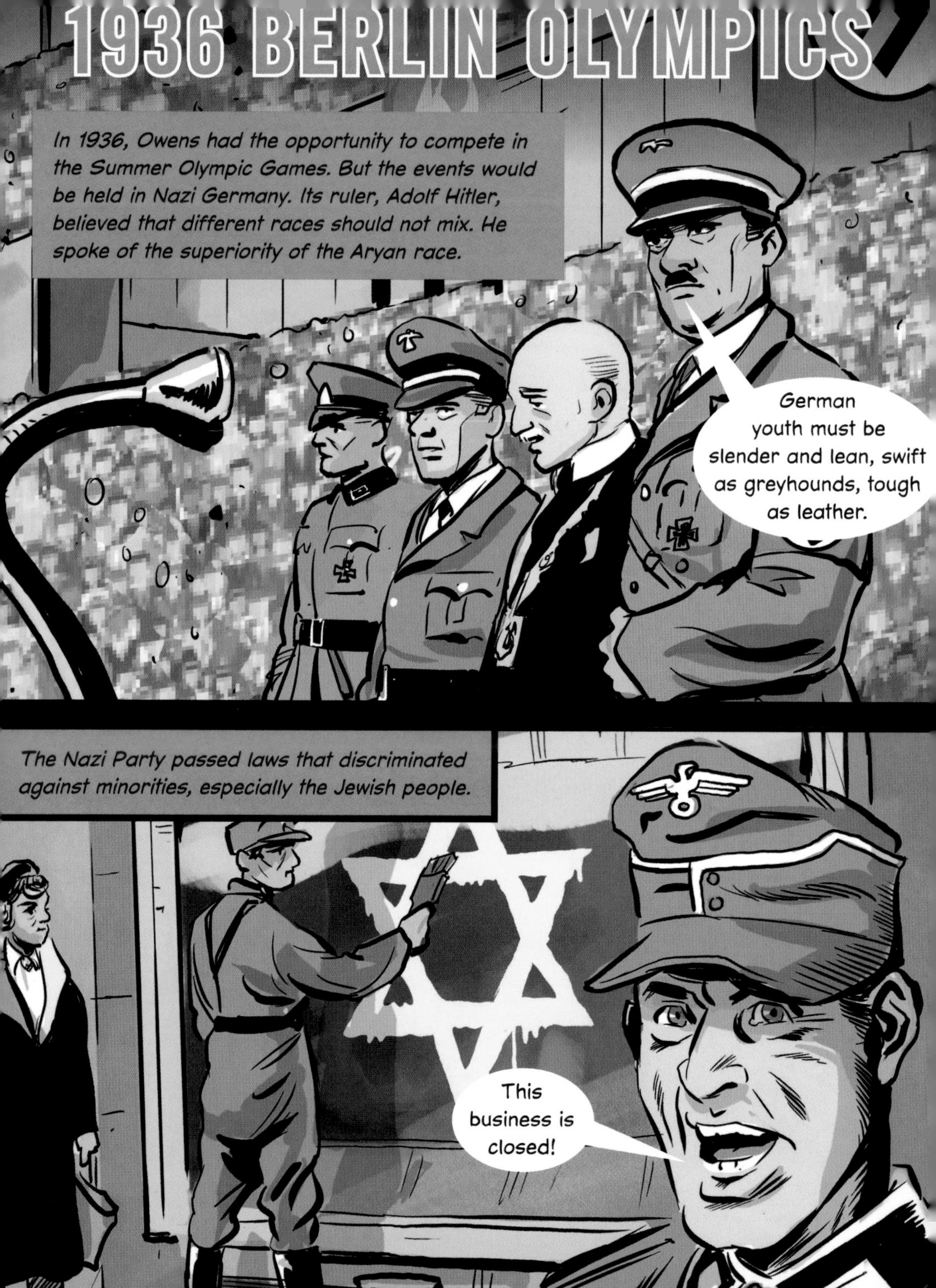
1936 BERLIN OLYMPICS
In 1936, Owens had the opportunity to compete in the Summer Olympic Games. But the events would be held in Nazi Germany. Its ruler, Adolf Hitler, believed that different races should not mix. He spoke of the superiority of the Aryan race.
German youth must be slender and lean, swift as greyhounds, tough as leather.
The Nazi Party passed laws that discriminated against minorities, especially the Jewish people.
This business is closed!

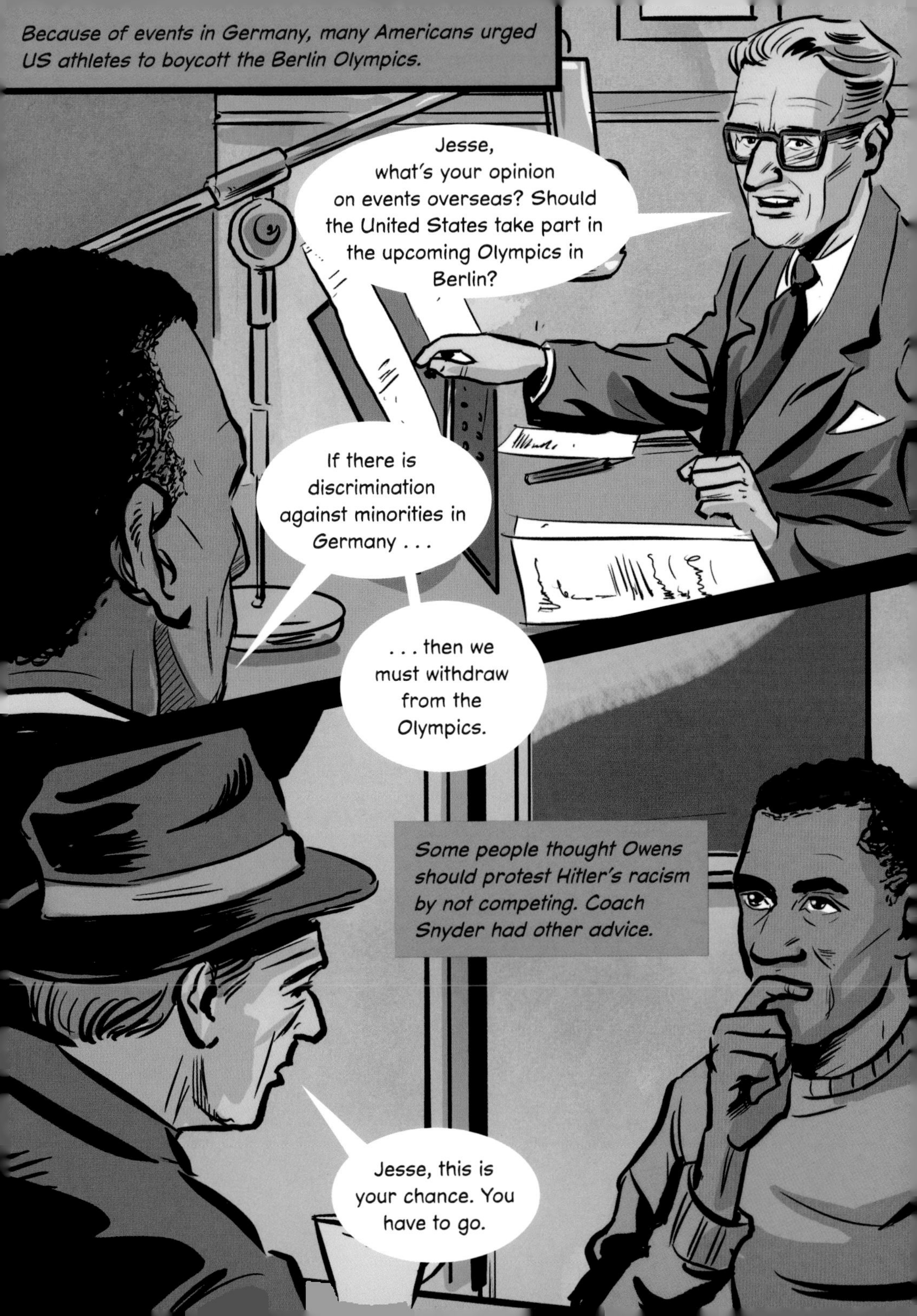
Because of events in Germany, many Americans urged US athletes to boycott the Berlin Olympics.
Jesse, what's your opinion on events overseas? Should the United States take part in the upcoming Olympics in Berlin?
If there is discrimination against minorities in Germany . . .
. . . then we must withdraw from the Olympics.
Some people thought Owens should protest Hitler's racism by not competing. Coach Snyder had other advice.
Jesse, this is your chance. You have to go.

The United States did not boycott the games. In July 1936, its Olympic team set sail for Berlin, Germany. The team included 18 African American athletes.

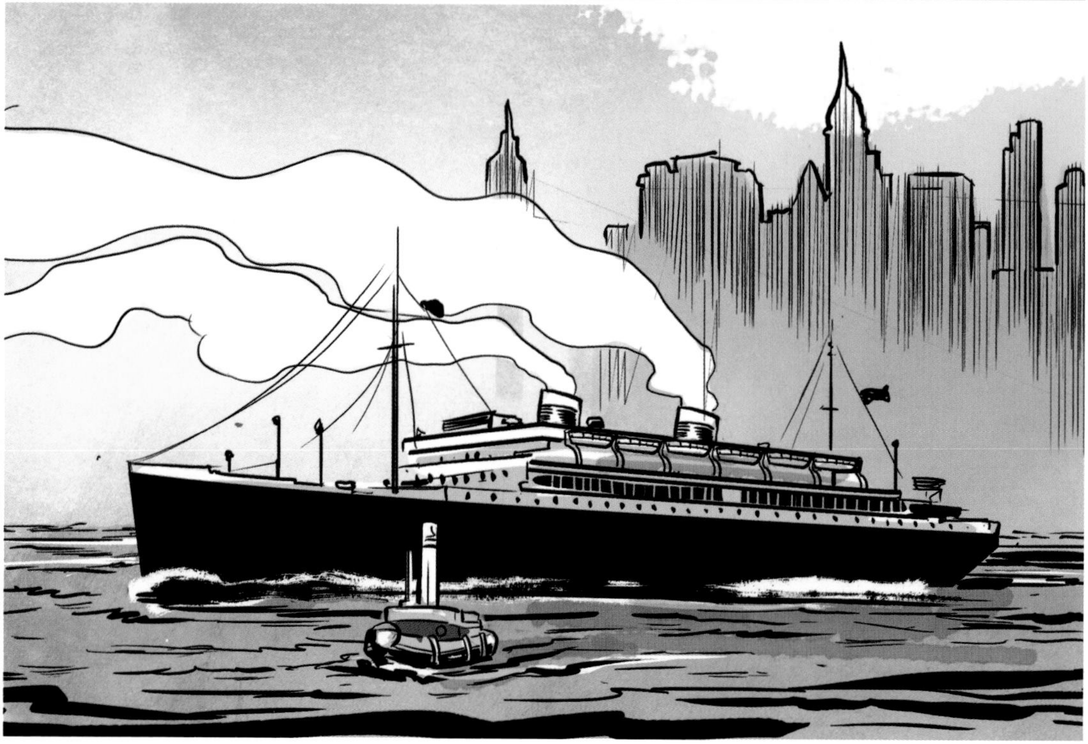

On August 1, the games began. Nearly 100,000 fans filled Berlin's Olympic Stadium as the athletes marched onto the field.

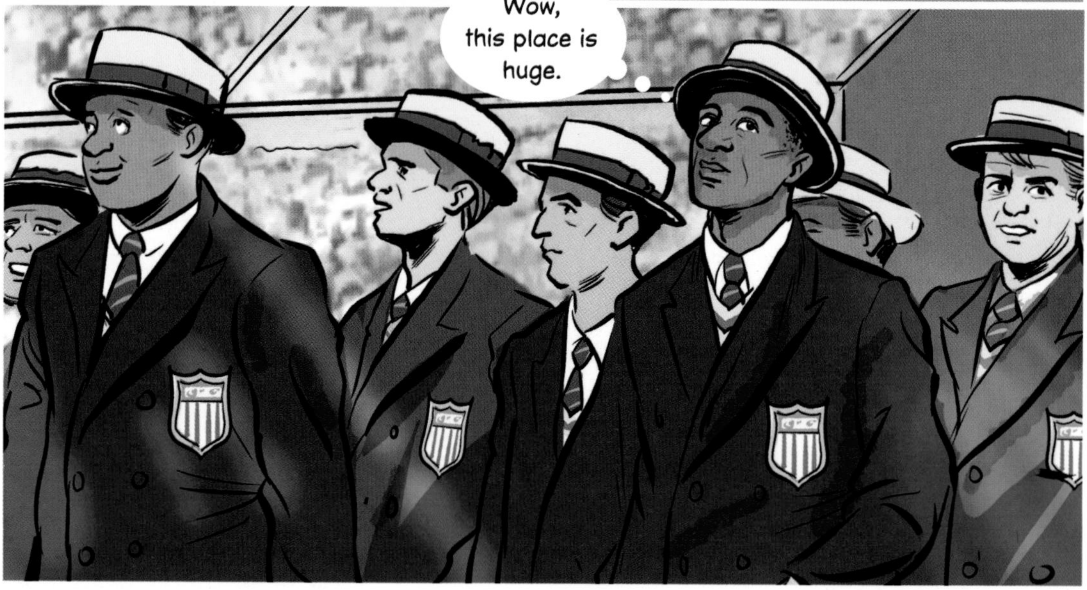
Wow, this place is huge.

The 100-meter final was held on day two of the games. This was Owens' moment.

Racers, on your mark.

Hitler and the Nazis hoped the Olympic Games would prove the superiority of the Aryan race.

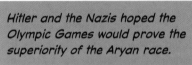

But Owens had other plans.

Owens is already in front!

Winner of the 100 meters, Jesse Owens!

He won with a time of 10.3 seconds.

The competition was grand. I was very glad to come out on top. Thank you very kindly.

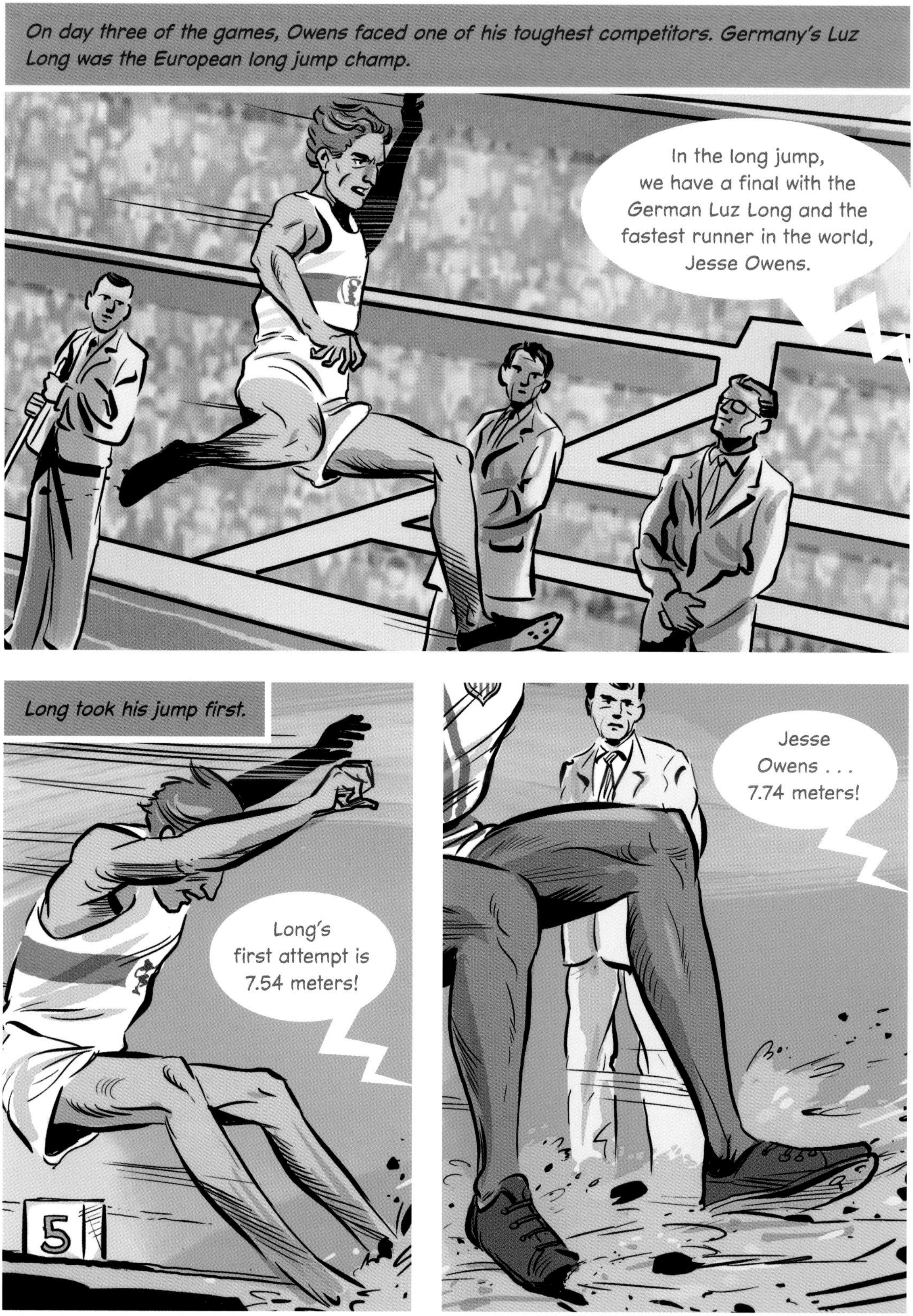
On day three of the games, Owens faced one of his toughest competitors. Germany's Luz Long was the European long jump champ.
In the long jump, we have a final with the German Luz Long and the fastest runner in the world, Jesse Owens.
Long took his jump first.
Long's first attempt is 7.54 meters!
5
Jesse Owens . . . 7.74 meters!

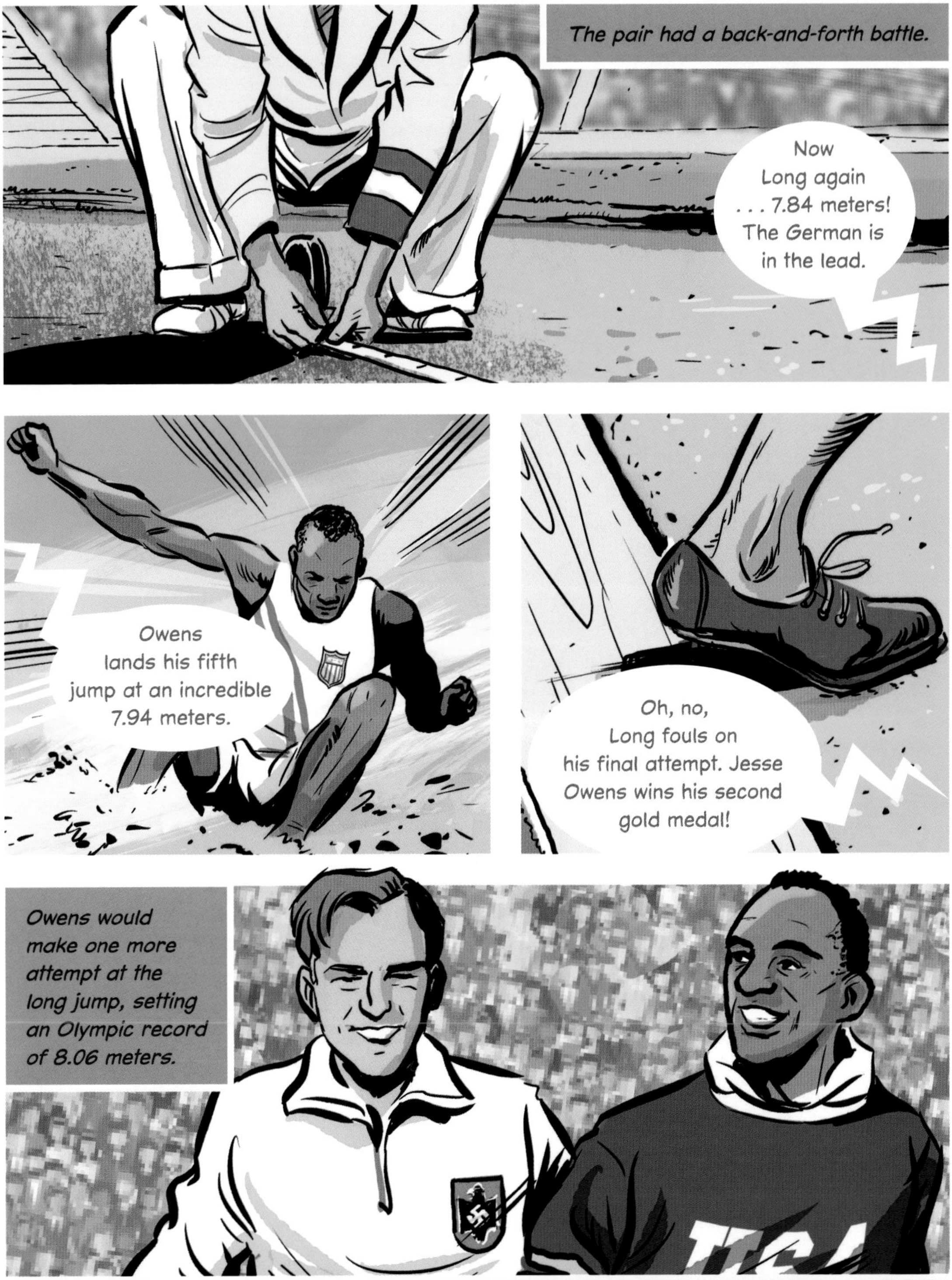

The pair had a back-and-forth battle.
Now Long again . . . 7.84 meters! The German is in the lead.
Owens lands his fifth jump at an incredible 7.94 meters.
Oh, no, Long fouls on his final attempt. Jesse Owens wins his second gold medal!
Owens would make one more attempt at the long jump, setting an Olympic record of 8.06 meters.
Competition brought Owens and Long together as friends. They stayed in touch until Long's death during World War II.

On day four of the games, Owens was back on the track. He competed in the finals for the 200-meter dash.

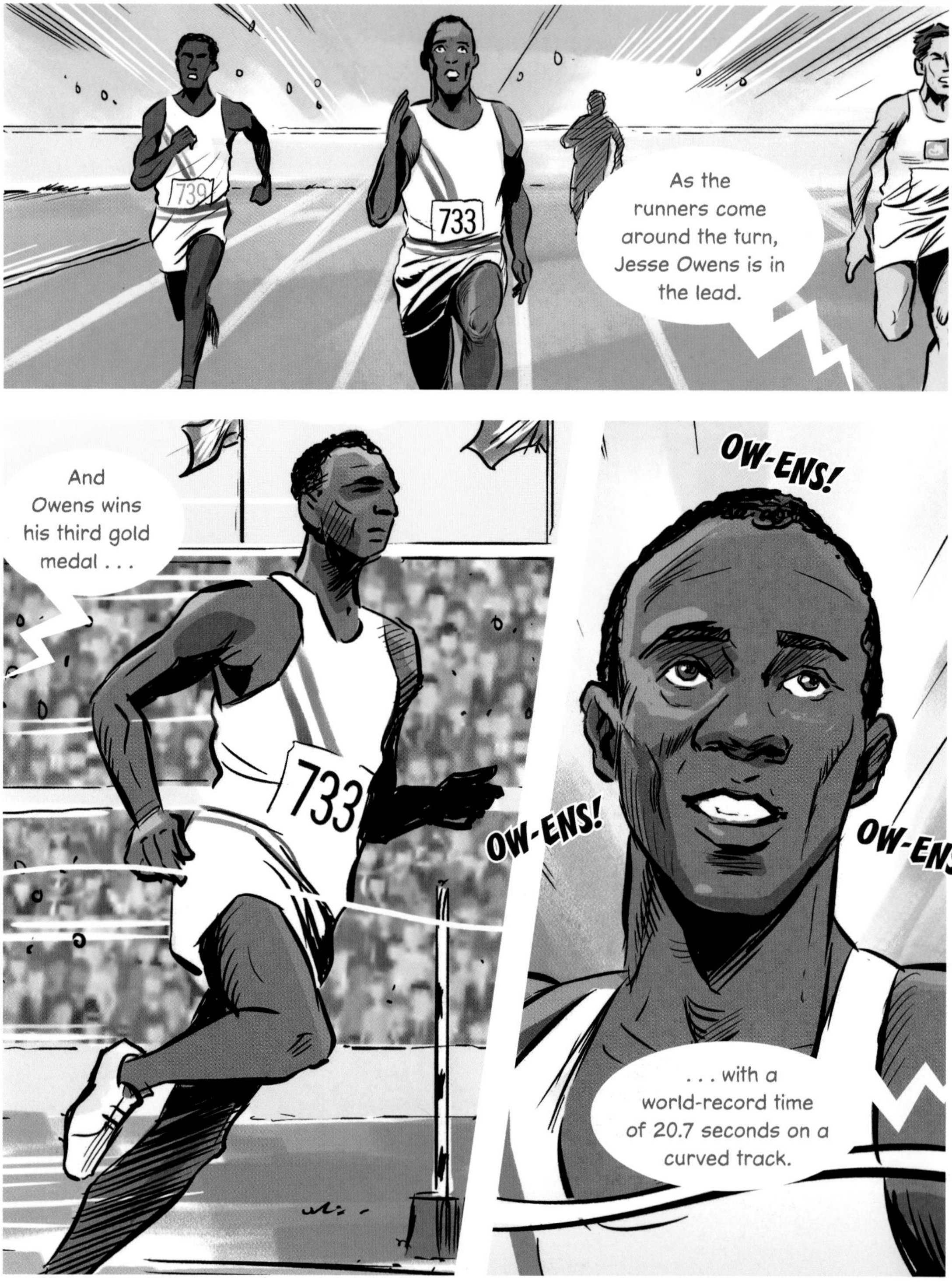

As the runners come around the turn, Jesse Owens is in the lead.
And Owens wins his third gold medal . . .
OW-ENS!
OW-ENS!
OW-ENS!
. . . with a world-record time of 20.7 seconds on a curved track.

Owens thought he was done competing after winning three gold medals. But the US track coaches had him run the 4x100-meter relay.

Owens, the fastest man in the world, puts America easily in the lead.

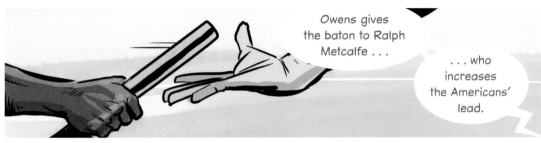

Owens gives the baton to Ralph Metcalfe . . .

. . . who increases the Americans' lead.

And the Americans win gold with a record time of 39.8 seconds.

Owens won four gold medals at the 1936 Olympics and was said to be the fastest man on Earth.

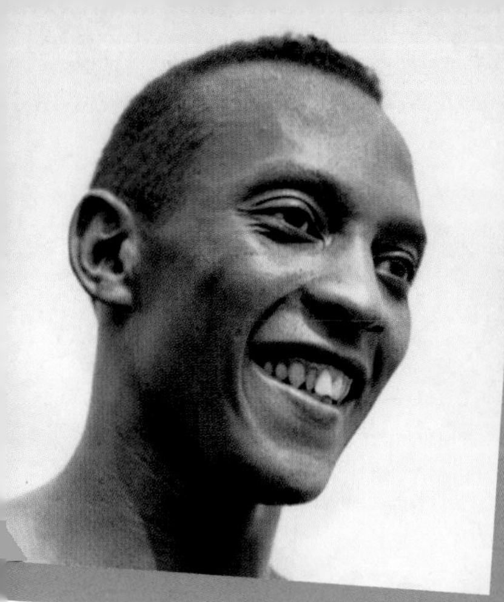

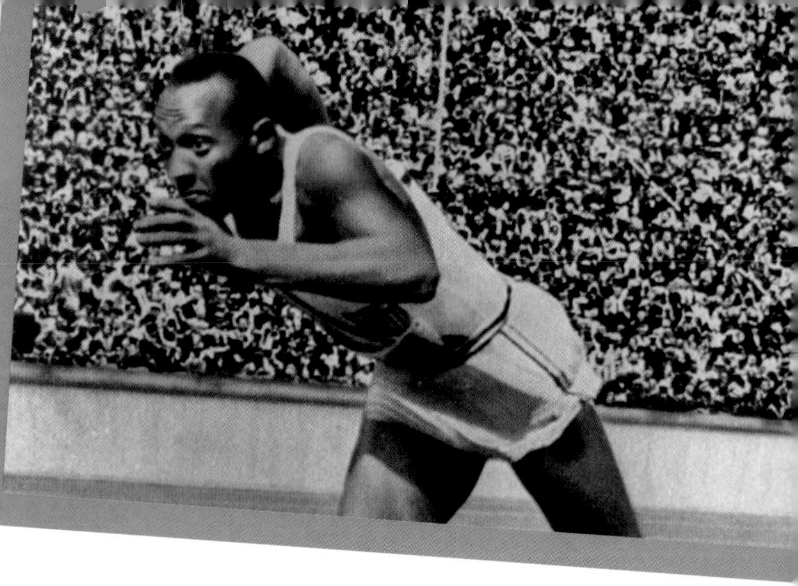

AFTERWORD

Upon his return home, Owens was an American hero. But he still faced discrimination. After the 1936 Olympics, President Franklin D. Roosevelt invited white US athletes to the White House. Owens and the other black athletes never received an invitation.

Owens had faced racism throughout his life. But on the running track, only speed mattered. Owens used the track to prove that he, like any person of color, had the power to win.

In 1980, Owens died from lung cancer. But his feats at the 1936 Olympic Games have not been forgotten. Owens is remembered for defying the racism of Nazi Germany through his athletic performance. He remains known as one of the greatest Olympic athletes of all time.

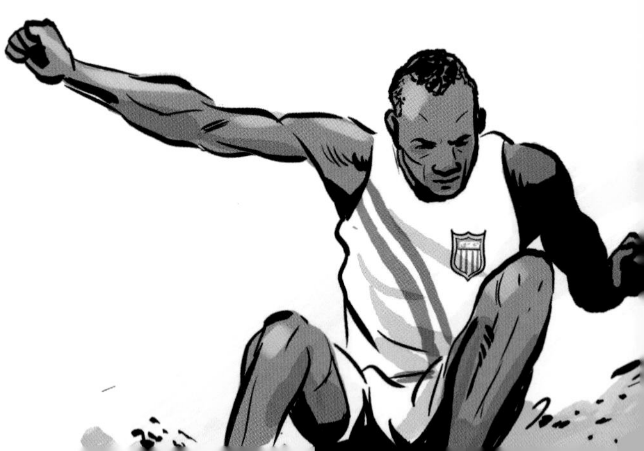

ATHLETE SNAPSHOT

BIRTH NAME: James Cleveland Owens

NICKNAMES: J.C., Jesse, Buckeye Bullet

BORN: September 12, 1913, Oakville, Alabama

DIED: March 31, 1980 (age 66), Tucson, Arizona

Awards of Note

- ◆ 1936 Olympic Games—four gold medals
- ◆ 1936—Associated Press Athlete of the Year (Male)
- ◆ 1976—Presidential Medal of Freedom
- ◆ 1983—US Olympic Hall of Fame
- ◆ 1990—Congressional Gold Medal

SOURCE NOTES

20   Laurens Grant, *American Experience: Jesse Owens*, PBS, 2012.

21   Jeremy Schaap, *Triumph: The Untold Story of Jesse Owens and Hitler's Olympics*. Boston: Houghton Mifflin, 2007.

23   Beny Lope, "Jesse Owens at the Berlin Olympics in 1936," YouTube video, 15:18, May 24, 2016, https://www.youtube.com /watch?v=1inifMJ0xio.

23–27   Leni Riefenstahl, *Olympia*, 1938 documentary translated from German to English.

GLOSSARY

Aryan: relating to non-Jewish, white Europeans

discriminate: to treat a person or group differently from other people or groups

migration: the act of moving from one place to another. The Great Migration refers to the relocation of millions of African Americans from 1916 to 1970. They sought to escape racial discrimination in the South and find better opportunities in the North.

racism: the belief that some races of people are better than others

sharecropper: a farmer who lives on and works land owned by someone else. The farmer receives some money from the sale of the crops while the landowner gets the rest.

FURTHER INFORMATION

Gitlin, Martin. *The 100 Greatest American Athletes*. Lanham, MD: Rowman & Littlefield, 2018.

Jesse Owens: Olympic Legend
http://www.jesseowens.com

Kortemeier, Todd. *12 Reasons to Love Track and Field*. Mankato, MN: 12 Story Library, 2018.

Olympic–Jesse Owens
https://www.olympic.org/jesse-owens

Stanmyre, Jackie F. *Jesse Owens: Facing Down Hitler*. New York: Cavendish Square, 2016.

Williams, Heather. *Jesse Owens*. Ann Arbor, MI: Cherry Lake Publishing, 2019.

INDEX